Contents

Front cover flap
Resplendent in an ivory gown, embroidered with the emblems of the United Kingdom and wearing George IV's diamond circlet Queen Elizabeth II arrives at Westminster Abbey for her coronation on 2 June 1953. The Queen retains this diamond-encrusted circlet (see page 59) in her personal collection, and wears it frequently.

Opposite
Detail from the Imperial Crown of India, 1911 (see page 49).

Right
Sovereign's Sceptre containing the famous Cullinan I diamond (see page 40).

Cover
The Imperial State Crown, 1937 (see page 34).

The whole theatre of coronation captured in Westminster Abbey in 1953 by Terence Cuneo. The Duke of Edinburgh is the first noble to pay homage to Queen Elizabeth II. Homage is the final part of the coronation where the nobility swears allegiance to the newly crowned sovereign.

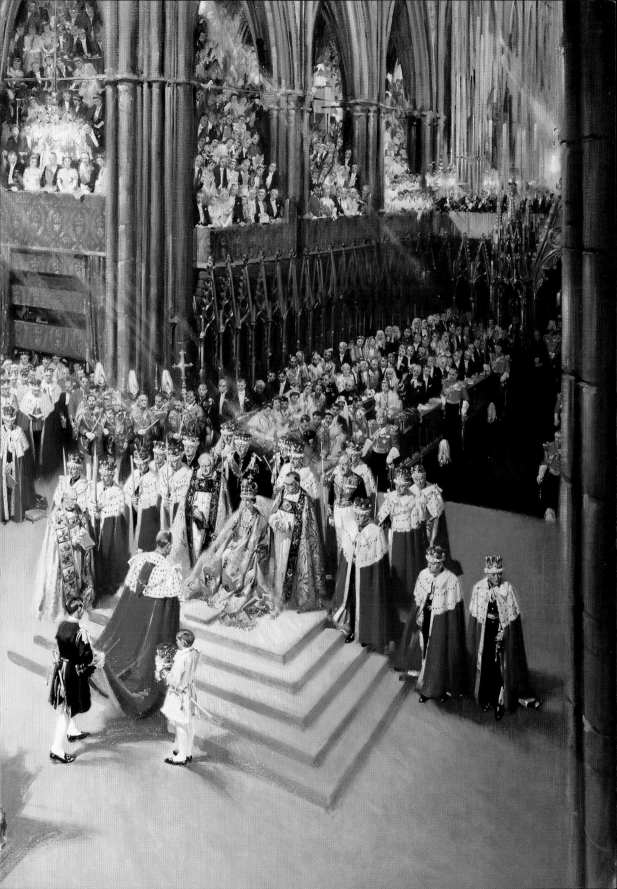

Introduction

In Britain, you see royal crowns everywhere. On postboxes, mail vans and beer glasses, printed on tax returns and carved on to government buildings, in corporate logos and history books. The crown is like a 'brand' for monarchy, and for Britain, which remains a constitutional monarchy with The Queen as Head of State. All these crowns are symbols of the power of the State, and they underline just how ancient that power is.

There are also crowns – and many other precious symbols of monarchy – that are real objects: the Crown Jewels in the Tower of London. This guidebook gives you many and varied insights into the gorgeous trappings of monarchy that are on display: their history, their manufacture, their symbolism, and the ceremonies for which they were made.

Opposite
The Imperial State Crown, 1937.
This is one of the most hard-working stars of the coronation regalia, worn by the sovereign at the conclusion of the coronation service and on occasions of state throughout the reign.

Crowning glory

Why do kings and queens wear crowns? In the Old Testament, kings were crowned with some sort of gold band. That tradition was revived in grander style by the Byzantine emperors who ruled from Constantinople (now Istanbul). It was taken up again by the European rulers who converted to Christianity after the Western Roman Empire had fallen. Non-Christian kings in the Dark Ages, such as the 7th-century Anglo-Saxon king (possibly Rædwald) who was buried in such splendour at Sutton Hoo in Suffolk, usually had elaborate and ornate helmets as their symbols of power. In all cases, these were incredibly valuable objects, made with the highest level of skill, using precious metals and some set with precious stones.

Over time, these crowns became ever more elaborate. Kings had a crown for everyday use, and the coronation crown that was worn rarely but was the ultimate symbol of their sacred and regal authority. England's medieval kings wore gold circlets embellished with stylized flowers, but from the 13th century the crown actually used in the coronation ceremony had arches that crossed over the head of the monarch. A monde, or mini-orb, above the arches symbolises that only God is above the monarch, who has no higher earthly power above him or her. The crowns were accompanied by other symbols of power: a sceptre indicating control over the realm and royal rights; a rod representing the responsibility to protect the people; a sword for military strength; and an orb – a globe representing the world with a cross on top symbolising God's power over all creation.

The earliest detailed account of a coronation in England comes from 973, when the Anglo-Saxon king Edgar was crowned in a lavish ceremony at Bath. The coronation rituals, last witnessed in 1953 when Queen Elizabeth II was crowned at Westminster, have altered little in their essentials in those thousand years. The monarch swears an oath to uphold the Church, to rule with wisdom and with mercy. The monarch is anointed on the head and body with a holy oil. The investiture follows: a ring, a sword, a rod or sceptre, an orb and a crown. A communion service follows, and all those in the coronation church swear loyalty to the new monarch. After a solemn procession and presentation to the people, there is traditionally a great feast, although the last one was held in 1821.

Since 1066, the coronation ceremony has taken place with very few exceptions in Westminster Abbey, the great church originally built by Edward the Confessor, who was buried there in that year (and where his saintly shrine remains). Westminster has had a central place in royal, parliamentary and government history since that memorable date.

Above
The coronation of Henry III depicted in a 13th-century manuscript. From the coronation of Henry III in 1220 to the mid-17th century, English monarchs were crowned with ornaments said to have belonged to Edward the Confessor.

Opposite
Charles I by Daniel Mytens, 1631 (detail) showing the imperial crown probably made for Henry VII after his victory at Bosworth. It was melted down at the Tower after Charles was executed.

The 'trifles' of monarchy

Until 1649, the coronation regalia – the crown and these other sacred and precious symbols of monarchy – were kept at Westminster. The 'ordinary' crowns travelled with the monarch, and sometimes these were stored alongside other rare and valuable possessions at the Tower of London. Since its construction, the royal stronghold has been a secure place to keep the nation's valuables, whether they be arms and armour, political prisoners, coins and minting equipment, state archives, or treasure.

It was in 1649 that the coronation regalia were brought to the Tower – to be destroyed. Charles I had been executed after the civil wars that had wracked the British Isles, a republic was declared, and the 'trifles' of monarchy were melted down. Some of the jewels worn by earlier kings and queens escaped the destruction, while some items were sold off. The Coronation Spoon and the Swords of Spiritual Justice, Temporal Justice and Mercy survive (see pages 20 and 14 respectively) and can be seen at the Tower of London today.

The 'new' Crown Jewels

In 1660 Charles II was restored to the throne, and the ancient ceremonies were revived. A new set of coronation regalia had to be made, and Charles was crowned in splendour in 1661. The ritual of coronation may be ancient, but the objects still in use are relatively modern. The regalia made in 1660-61 have been re-fashioned in various ways since that date, not least to display the huge diamond discovered in Africa a century and more ago, and they have been added to over the course of time. William III and Mary II, as joint monarchs, needed matching regalia. George IV, who was crowned in one the most gorgeous ceremonies ever witnessed at Westminster, spent hugely, adding to the Jewel House. Alongside the Crown of St Edward, only ever used for the coronation, the Imperial State Crown, for regular use on occasions such as the State Opening of Parliament, was remade in 1937. The celebrated Koh-i-Nûr, the diamond for which Eastern rulers had once schemed, fought and killed (see page 49), has been incorporated in turn into three of the crowns worn by queens consort (wives of ruling kings). George V's crown as Emperor of India, containing thousands of diamonds, was only ever worn once, at the Delhi Durbar of 1911 (see page 51). The Jewel House displays traditionally include the altar plate and baptismal fonts used on royal occasions, objects used in the various stages of the ceremonial, and items used for coronation banquets, including the vast wine cooler made for George IV (see page 57). Other items date from 1953, when there was a conscious search for antique precedents to use in the coronation of Queen Elizabeth II.

Jewels at the Tower

The Crown Jewels have been in their present, highly secure, home on the ground floor of the Waterloo Barracks since 1994, having been previously located in the basement of that building from 1967. When the new regalia were made in 1661, they were kept initially in the old Tudor Jewel House, which stood against the south side of the White Tower. In 1669 the Crown Jewels were moved to the Lower Martin Tower where the Jewel House shop is now located. It was here that the daring 'Colonel' Blood tried – and almost succeeded – to steal the Crown Jewels in 1671 (see page 68). A purpose-built Jewel House was constructed in 1842, which stood to the south of the Martin Tower. The pressure of people eager to view the Jewels, the need for greater security, and the desire to improve ways of displaying the objects, forced a further move, into the Upper Wakefield Tower in 1868. There they remained for a century.

In excess of 30 million people have seen the Crown Jewels in their present setting. These are among the most visited objects in Britain, perhaps in the world. They carry a mystique that far transcends their monetary value as gold, diamonds and other precious gems. They are sacred and profoundly symbolic objects. Their ancestry stretches back into biblical antiquity, and their national significance extends for over a millennium. But they are in essence a unique, working collection. When the next coronation comes, the contents of the Tower of London's Treasury will have been taken to Westminster. And visitors on a certain day in November each year, when Parliament is opened, will see a little notice in the showcase for the Imperial State Crown that says, 'In use'.

Opposite
Charles II (detail) by John Michael Wright *c*1661. The King holds the Sovereign's Sceptre with Cross and the Sovereign's Orb, made for him in 1661 and used at every coronation since.

Right
The Imperial State Crown, 1937, being carried at the State Opening of Parliament.

The Procession

Before the age of film and television, only a small number of people could watch the coronation service in Westminster Abbey, and so the processions that preceded and followed it were important ceremonial spectacles in their own right, allowing tens of thousands to witness something of the splendour and pomp of the occasion.

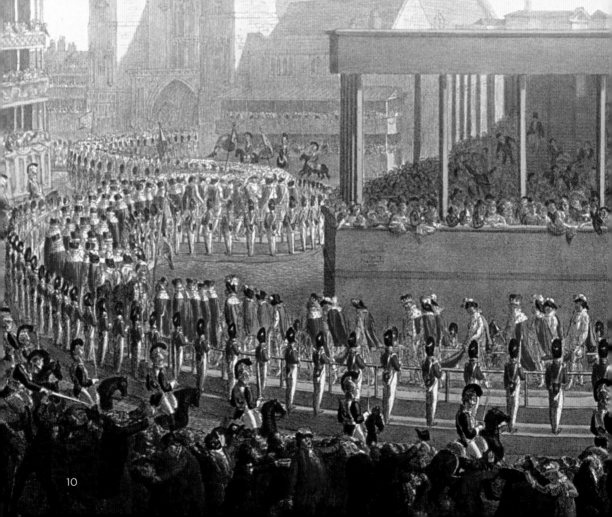

The coronation procession provided spectators with the sight of magnificent clothes, carriages and even some marvellous bit-part characters: the statuesque Queen of Tonga was a highlight of the procession in 1953, and in 1727 the spectacle included the outrageous Countess of Orkney, retired mistress of William III, exposing 'a mixture of fat and wrinkles' and 'a considerable pair of boobies a good deal withered'. There were usually musicians in the procession, including in 1603 'three windy musicians' whose instruments were sackbuts (a form of trombone). At George II's coronation in 1727, the exhausted Duchess of Marlborough made use of a temporary pause to grab and sit upon a drum.

For over 300 years the coronation procession used to start at the Tower of London before snaking its way to the Palace of Westminster and the Abbey.

Occasionally it was called off: James I and Charles I cancelled theirs, officially because of the plague, with James postponing his until the following year. From 1685, the procession started closer to the Abbey, but the Tower was still involved: by this time the regalia that would be used in the ceremony could be seen on display there by anyone who cared to visit.

The king or queen to be crowned wears red parliamentary robes for the procession into the Abbey (and purple imperial robes on the way out). Since the 20th century, once the procession reaches the Abbey some of its members pick up and carry the various regalia. The exciting, closing stage of the procession, up the nave of the Abbey, therefore, gives a glimpse of some very important treasures that are used in the ceremony itself.

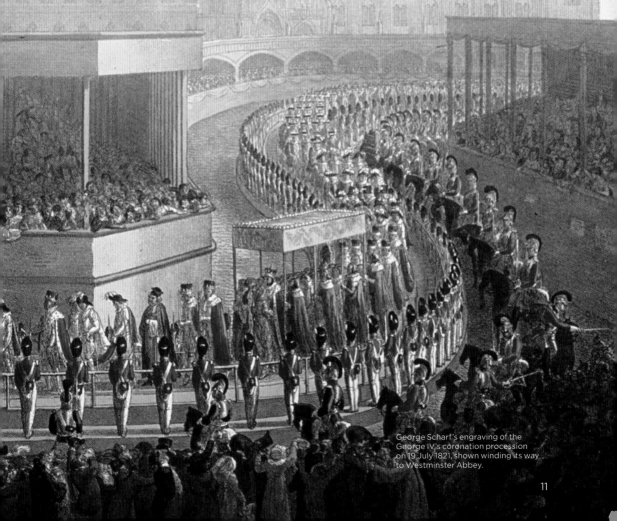

George Scharf's engraving of the George IV's coronation procession on 19 July 1821, shown winding its way to Westminster Abbey.

The Maces

You could do a lot of damage with a functional mace: it was a metal club bristling with spikes. Whirled around the head of the medieval knight it was a fearsome weapon.

But the ten maces displayed in the Jewel House today are ornamental rather than dangerous. They are carried by the Sergeants at Arms, or the royal bodyguard. For Charles II's coronation procession in 1661, all 13 of them had a new mace, and while their weapons were ceremonial they still nevertheless fulfilled their traditional security function. During a chapel procession one of them spotted 'the glittering of a sword' in the crowd, and seized a 'naked' blade from a would-be assassin.

Over time, the mace has also become the symbol of royal authority in Parliament and a further three are on permanent loan to the Palace of Westminster: two (one held in reserve) for the House of Lords and one for the Commons. The mace precedes the arrival and departure of the Speaker from the chamber and neither house can lawfully meet without the mace present.

The Sword of State, 1678

The sword received by the sovereign during the coronation ceremony (the Jewelled Sword of Offering – see page 21) is represented after the event by another sword that is carried sheathed before him or her on all formal occasions. This was initially any sword, rather than a specific weapon, until the Sword of State was 'most Extraordinary wrought' for Charles II in 1660, and a second made in 1678 so that one could be used in Parliament and one in palaces. This sword may still be seen out and about and doing its work: being carried before The Queen at the State Opening of Parliament, for example, or at other great state events.

The Irish Sword of State, c1660

British kings and queens did not very often visit Ireland when it was under their rule and were represented there by their Lords Lieutenant. When the Lord Lieutenant was standing in for the monarch on Irish state occasions, the Irish Sword of State did symbolic duty for the Sword of State (above). The sword was ordered in 1660 and was carried before the Lord Lieutenant of Ireland in processions right up until 1922 and the formation of the Irish Free State, when it was 'retired' to the Jewel House.

St Edward's Staff, 1661

One consequence of the great upheavals of the Civil War was the destruction of most of the regalia: '... now Edward's Staff is broken, chair overturned, Clothes rent, and Crown melted; our present Age esteeming them the Relics of Superstition'.

Englishmen believed that the original St Edward's Staff was the property of medieval saint-king Edward the Confessor. Although it was not needed in the actual coronation ceremony, it was carried in the procession as a holy relic. When Charles II ordered a new set of regalia in the 1660s, a replacement staff was included, and you see it here today.

People have always found it tempting to exaggerate its antiquity and sanctity. Many in the 18th century believed it was still St Edward's medieval original, and some Victorian guidebooks even claimed that it contained a 'fragment of the true cross'.

Opposite left
One of 13 ceremonial maces dating from the 17th century. Each mace measures about 1.5m (4.9ft) in length and weighs around 10kg (22lb).

Opposite right
Detail from an engraving of James II's coronation procession of 1685 showing a Sergeant at Arms bearing a ceremonial mace in the traditional manner.

This page (from left to right)
The Sword of State, 1678. The richly decorated hilt and scabbard are designed to be seen when the sword is held point upwards, as traditionally carried before the monarch.

The Irish Sword of State, c1660. Used by the Lord Lieutenant of Ireland, this sword represented the authority of the absent monarch.

St. Edward's Staff, 1661, was carried in the coronation procession as a holy relic.

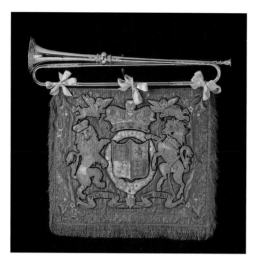

The State Trumpets

Westminster Abbey has notoriously poor sight lines and most coronation guests cannot actually see the crowning. Splendid and stirring music – an important part of royal ceremonial – compensates in part.

Trumpets, the traditional instruments for fanfares and signals, punctuate the whole service: they sounded, for example, at the moment that St Edward's Crown was lowered on to the head of Queen Elizabeth II in 1953. In 1603 the trumpeters were stationed all round the Abbey, to create a complex effect of calls and answers. The 11 silver trumpets now displayed in the Jewel House were used for various ceremonies between 1780 and 1848, and many are engraved with the name of the particular trumpeter who played them.

The Swords of Spiritual Justice, Temporal Justice and Mercy (the Curtana)

The sword, an essential weapon for any knight, had firmly arrived as part of the coronation ritual by the 10th century, at the dawn of the age of chivalry. The sword symbolised a king's physical strength, and his prowess in defending church and people. Swords in Arthurian romances almost became characters in their own right, and so too did the Swords of Justice and Mercy.

The Sword of Mercy or 'Curtana' has a particularly stirring history. What we see today is a replacement of a medieval sword that was believed to have belonged in turn to the Arthurian hero Tristan; to Morhaut, champion of Ireland; and to Emperor Charlemagne.

All three swords are carried unsheathed, pointing upwards, in the coronation procession. Similar swords were part of Richard I's procession as early as 1189: perhaps they stood for his three realms of England, Anjou and Normandy. Later on they developed an extra layer of meaning: the Swords of Spiritual Justice and Temporal Justice are sharp and vengeful, while the Sword of Mercy is blunt and benevolent. The swords actually used in 1189 are long lost, and their replacements date from the early 17th century. They were probably supplied for the coronation of Charles I in 1626.

The three swords (seen opposite in the procession for the Coronation of George V) are specially significant because, with the exception of the Coronation Spoon, they are the only pieces to have survived the great destruction of precious royal objects after the Civil War.

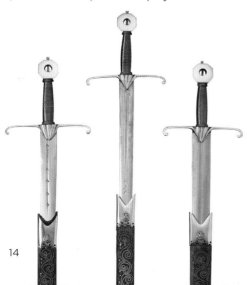

Above
A silver state trumpet, with its richly embroidered banner made for Queen Victoria in 1838.

Left
The Swords of Temporal Justice, Spiritual Justice and Mercy, c1626 are a highly symbolic feature of the coronation procession.

Opposite
The Coronation of George V in Westminster Abbey, 22nd June 1911 (detail) by JHF Bacon, 1911, clearly showing the Swords of Temporal Justice, Spiritual Justice and Mercy (the Curtana).

'Be ye a good knight'

An ancient ceremony involving a ritual bath prepared the 'Knights of the Bath' for the honour of escorting a new monarch to his coronation.

The bathing ceremony (symbolising purification) took place the day before the coronation procession left the Tower of London. The first recorded ceremony at the Tower was before Henry IV's coronation in 1399, when 46 knights were created.

These manuscript illuminations were created in the 15th century and show just how solemn, joyous (and sometimes rather uncomfortable) the transformation from squire to knight could be.

The squire is greeted at the royal lodgings. Two 'governor-squires' will guide him throughout his initiation.

The squire is led to his chamber in the White Tower (right). Here, a bath is prepared for him, lined in white linen, and covered with thick carpets to keep out the cold. The squire is undressed and sits in his bath, whilst a solemn group of experienced knights each pours a handful of water on his shoulder, and gives him advice about his knightly duties. A bed has been prepared, and he lies down for a while to dry off.

The squire's ordeal must continue though and, as night begins, he cannot rest. On to the next stage – the vigil. The vigil would take place sometimes in St John's Chapel in the White Tower, or in St Peter's on Tower Green. There, the squire is left to pray and contemplate knighthood until morning. After his sleepless night he can at last rest and, cleansed by prayer, he returns to his bed. Not for long though...

The squire is awoken by singing and trumpeting minstrels, and is dressed by his governor-squires. He is led to the king's hall on horseback, escorted by wise knights and heralds and the music of the minstrels. A finely-dressed youth proudly carries the squire's sword for him.

In the hall, trusted knights put spurs on the squire's heels. The king attaches the sword to the squire's belt. The squire raises his arms and the monarch strikes him on the neck with his right hand and says 'Be ye a good knight', and kisses him. The blow on the neck is to remind the squire of the seriousness of his commitment, and his fate should he fail in his duty.

The new knight is led away to the chapel to give thanks. Here the master cook cuts off his spurs! This reminds the knight of the humiliation he will suffer if he fails to behave in a knightly fashion. The knight returns to sit at the king's feast. After enduring a cold bath and a sleepless night, he must not eat, and has to sit silently at the king's table, observing all around him.

Afterwards, the sleep-deprived and famished knight can retire to his chamber to eat, and there he is dressed in the fine blue robes that proclaim him a Knight of the Bath. Now he is ready, and can proudly escort his monarch on the processional route from the Tower to Westminster Abbey.

The last occasion on which Knights of the Bath were created with full bathing ceremony was the coronation of Charles II in 1661. In 1725 George I founded the 'Most Honourable Military Order of the Bath', based upon the name of that ancient ritual. A version of the order still operates today, with the sovereign at its head and the Prince of Wales as its Grand Master. Members of the Order are now usually senior military officers or senior civil servants.

Charles II's coronation regalia, attributed to Pieter Gerritsz van Roestraeten (1629-1700), showing the Sovereign's Sceptre before the mighty diamond Cullinan I was added to its head by George V for his coronation in 1911.

The Anointing and Investiture

The ceremony of coronation is a Christian service. For many centuries the new monarch was considered to be divinely appointed, and the ceremony shares many similarities with the consecration of a bishop.

The coronation begins with the Recognition, as the people – represented by the congregation – shout their acceptance of the monarch, and in response he or she pledges an oath before God to rule fairly and protect the Church. Then follows the second unique part of the ceremony, the Anointing and Investiture – rites that can be traced in England as far back as the 9th-century Anglo-Saxon kings.

The Anointing

The Archbishop of Canterbury, who leads the service, pours an aromatic holy oil from the **Ampulla**, 1661, an ornamental flask, into the ancient **Coronation Spoon**, 12th century, and anoints the monarch on the hands, breast and head. This special form of holy blessing has both biblical and pagan origins. The gold Ampulla, supplied to Charles II by his goldsmith Robert Vyner, was a replacement of the much smaller, medieval original destroyed in 1649. This also took the form of an eagle and it was believed to contain oil given to St Thomas Becket by the Virgin Mary and used at several coronations from the 15th century. The spoon of silver-gilt is the only survival held at the Tower of London from the medieval regalia and was listed in an inventory at the Abbey in 1359 even then as being 'of ancient form'. It is also the only piece of royal goldsmith's work to survive from the 12th century, with its characteristic handle, decorated with intricate leafy arabesques and a monster's head. The spoon avoided being melted down during the Civil War because it was bought by Clement Kynnersley, who served in both Charles I's and Cromwell's Wardrobes (the department responsible for royal furniture) and returned it at the Restoration.

Above left
Ampulla, 1661. At 20.6cm (8.1in) tall, this ornamental gold flask in the form of an eagle contains an aromatic holy oil known as chrism. The oil is poured from the eagle's beak.

Left
Coronation Spoon, 12th century. This elegant anointing spoon, 26.7cm (10.5in) long, is the only surviving relic from the medieval regalia.

The Coronation Robes

These robes were last worn by Queen Elizabeth II at the coronation in 1953. The outer robes are based on ancient imperial vestments and are woven from silk thread wound round with gold. In appearance, they are similar to the robes of high-ranking clergy, emphasising the sovereign's divinely sanctioned rule.

Over the monarch's linen shift (the colobium sidonis) is worn the **Supertunica**, 1911, a long coat of cloth-of-gold that was made for George V but is almost identical to the earliest known design made for James II in 1685.

Next the priestly **Stole**, 1953, is placed around the neck. This most recent version bears the emblems of the British Isles and for the first time, symbolic plants of the Commonwealth. Finally the oldest and most impressive garment is put on, the **Imperial Mantle**, 1821, which was made for George IV's coronation and was used by the present Queen in 1953. Like his Jewelled Sword of Offering, this is covered in the emblems of the newly created United Kingdom, along with imperial eagles that recall the ancient origins of the mantle.

The Investiture

The Investiture of the monarch begins with the **Coronation Robes** (see page 21). Once robed, the monarch receives a series of ornaments that symbolise the chivalric aspects of kingship – the counterpart to its spiritual nature. First the **Spurs** made in 1660-1 (fabric strips, 1821) that are designed to echo their medieval predecessors. Originally the spurs were fastened to the sovereign's feet but since the Restoration they have been simply held to the ankles of kings and only presented to queens regnant.

Just as a new knight is invested by the monarch with a sword, the new monarch is presented with the **Jewelled Sword of Offering**, 1820, as has been recorded since long before the reign of James II. He or she is charged with protecting good and punishing evil. It is fastened about a king's waist, although queens do not wear the sword. It is then offered up at the altar and later redeemed for 100 shillings (£5.00) by the Keeper of the Jewel House. George IV ordered this magnificent sword from the Crown Jewellers, Rundell, Bridge and Rundell. Crowned the first 'King of the United Kingdom of Great Britain and Ireland', George IV was determined to use the emblems of the kingdom as much as possible at his coronation. The sword scabbard is set with gemstones in designs of the rose, thistle and shamrock.

The Armills of Charles II, 1661, are golden bracelets, similarly embellished with enamelled emblems of the kingdom. When they were remade at the Restoration their ancient symbolic associations with knighthood and military leadership were still understood, although their exact purpose in the ceremony had been lost and it seems that they had no ceremonial use. However, in 1953 the presentation of the armills was revived and the Commonwealth countries gave **Queen Elizabeth II** these new gold **Armills**, which she did wear at the coronation.

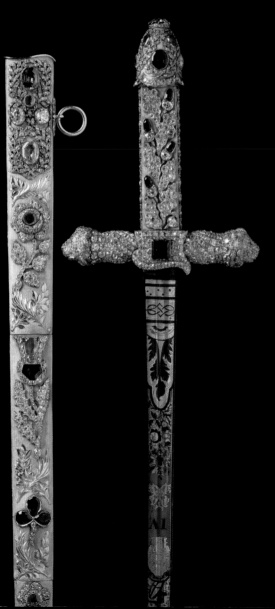

Left
The Jewelled Sword of Offering, 1820. This highly ornate sword, set with precious stones showing emblems of different parts of Britain, was made for the coronation of George IV.

Above
The Armills, 1953, called bracelets of sincerity and wisdom in the coronation ceremony itself.

Opposite
The Sovereign's Orb, 1661. The hollow gold orb is set with pearls, precious stones and a large amethyst.

The gold **Sovereign's Orb**, 1661, symbolises the Christian world with its cross mounted on a globe, and its bands of jewels and pearls dividing it up to represent the three continents known in medieval Europe. It is also an ancient emblem of imperial power, stretching back to Roman and the Byzantine – Christian – empires. The monarch receives it in the right hand before it is placed on the altar. Many of its gemstones are original.

The unique occasion of a joint coronation demanded a second orb for the queen regnant. **Queen Mary's Orb**, 1689, was made for the elder daughter of James II, when she took the throne with her Dutch husband William III in 1689. The orb was set with hired stones – as were other items from the regalia in the past – and some of the imitation stones that replaced these for display in the Jewel House are now over 300 years old.

The final part of the Investiture consists of the placing of the coronation ring on the fourth finger of the sovereign's right hand, and the receiving of the sceptre and rod. The **Sovereign's Ring**, 1831, was made for William IV with rubies forming the cross of St George (patron saint of England) on a large sapphire. Rubies have been used for the monarch's ring since medieval times and represent dignity. The **Queen Consort's Ring**, 1831, belonged to William's consort, Queen Adelaide, who for the first time bequeathed the coronation rings rather than retaining them personally. **Queen Victoria's Coronation Ring**, 1838, is a smaller version of William IV's, although due to a misunderstanding it was actually made too small and had to be forced on to her finger by the Archbishop.

Victoria noted in her diary 'I had the greatest difficulty to take it off again – which at last I did with great pain'. Queen Adelaide left her own and her husband's coronation rings to Queen Victoria, who in turn bequeathed them and her own ring to the Crown. All three rings were deposited in the Tower in 1919. The Sovereign's Ring has been used by every sovereign since 1902, and the Queen Consort's Ring by all queen consorts since that date.

The sceptre and rod have universal associations with military command and good governance, but there is a subtlety in the English coronation in having these two related ornaments.

Their significance was described at the coronation of William the Conqueror in 1066: 'For by the sceptre uprisings in the kingdom are controlled and the rod gathers and confines those men that stray', emphasising that the rod also symbolised the monarch's pastoral care of his people.

The **Sovereign's Sceptre with Cross**, 1661 (see page 42), has been used at every coronation since it was made for Charles II. It was transformed in 1910 for George V when he added the spectacular Cullinan I diamond (or First Star of Africa), which his father had been given by the Transvaal Government (see page 41). At 530.20 carats it still remains the largest colourless cut diamond in the world. The **Sovereign's Sceptre with Dove**, 1661, has an enamel dove with its wings open perched on its cross to represent the Holy Ghost. James II's consort, Mary of Modena, was the first queen after the Restoration to be crowned and so required the **Queen Consort's Sceptre with Cross** and **Ivory Rod with Dove**, 1685. Both have been used by queens consort ever since. **Queen Mary's Sceptre with Dove**, 1689, as a second sovereign's sceptre, was only needed for her unique joint coronation with William III.

Above
The Sovereign's Ring (left)
and the Queen Consort's Ring,
both 1831.

Opposite
(from left to right) The Queen
Consort's Ivory Rod with Dove,
1685; Queen Mary II's Sceptre with
Dove, 1689; the Queen Consort's
Sceptre with Cross, 1685.

'Most delectable and excellent musick'

Can you imagine a coronation ceremony without trumpets? Musicologist and conductor **Christopher Hogwood** describes the development of stirring stuff.

Most of us will recognise Handel's rousing anthem *Zadok the Priest*, played at every coronation since 1727. Before that, music for coronations ranged from plainchant for Richard III to Charles I's 'windy musicians'.

The commissioning of the coronation music represents not only an honour for the composer, but also an opportunity for the monarch to express a musical opinion. In 1727, George II gave the commission to Handel over the head of Maurice Greene, the organist to the Chapel Royal. As Westminster was considered a Royal Chapel, Greene would have by rights expected to receive the coronation commission as this task normally fell to the royal organist. However, according to his son, the King had 'forbad that wretched little, crooked, ill-natured, insignificant musician, and ordered that GF Handel should have that great honour'. Handel completed the writing in two weeks.

Above
Portrait of the celebrated composer, George Frederick Handel (1685-1759), by William Hoare.

Left
A fanfare played by state trumpets heralds key moments of the coronation ceremony.

The result of this royal veto was the most popular and longest-lasting coronation music yet composed: the unforgettable opening crescendo of *Zadok the Priest* has been heard at every coronation since 1727, and of Handel's other three anthems, the gentler arrangement *My heart is inditing* was perfectly calculated for the crowning of George's wife, Caroline. However, the event was obviously under-rehearsed; the Archbishop of Canterbury, who officiated, wrote in his programme after *The King shall rejoice*: 'the anthem all in confusion: all irregular in the music'.

Although coronations have been held in Westminster Abbey since 1066, no form of service is provided in the Anglican Church's Book of Common Prayer. In the ancient *Liber Regalis* the essentials of Oath, Anointment, Investiture, Enthronement and Homage are listed and we assume acclamation, bells and fanfares *en route*.

In 1483 Richard III was met with 'most delectable and excellent musick' and 'diverse songs solemply sung', surely plainchant; *Veni creator* has been sung at the Anointing since the reign of Richard II (1377-99).

With James I (1603), the Latin ceremony became an English service, and following the Restoration of Charles II (1661) more elaborate and organised music was included. A wooden gallery was erected in Westminster Abbey for the royal string band (the 'Twenty-four Violins') who accompanied the choir in settings by Lawes, Cooke and Child, while Matthew Locke wrote his *Music for his Majesties Sagbutts and Cornetts* for the procession from the Tower to Whitehall the previous day.

On the day, the procession from Westminster Hall to the Abbey (suspended for economic reasons by William IV in 1831) was a splendid array of more than 100 musicians, including trumpeters, drummers, flutes and 'singing men'. In the engraving of the procession for James II (1685) we find Henry Purcell marching with the choir; he also wrote his settings of *I was glad* and *My heart is inditing* for this ceremony.

At Queen Victoria's coronation in 1838 her uncles were criticised for beating time too noisily to Handel's familiar anthems. A special organ 'in the German manner' (with a full-compass pedal) was also built for this event, from which Sir George Smart directed a large band with the result, as the Press tartly put it, that 'there was no conductor'. Efficient control was now needed for the increasing number of musicians, from Queen Victoria's 400, to 500 for Edward VII (1902) and George V (1911). Hubert Parry's setting of *I was glad*, another favourite, first written for Edward VII in 1902, includes a section to accommodate the traditional shouts of 'Vivat Rex' (Long live the King!) by the scholars of Westminster School to greet the monarch.

For Queen Elizabeth II's coronation in June 1953, Vaughan Williams proposed an even more communal item and arranged the *Old 100th* (*All people that on earth do dwell*) for congregation, organ and orchestra; the remainder was a mix of old and new music by British (and one Commonwealth) composers, with six specially commissioned pieces.

Below
The rousing sound of trumpets, punctuated by the beat of a drum, fills the air as a group of musicians parade past in this image of the coronation procession of James II in 1685.

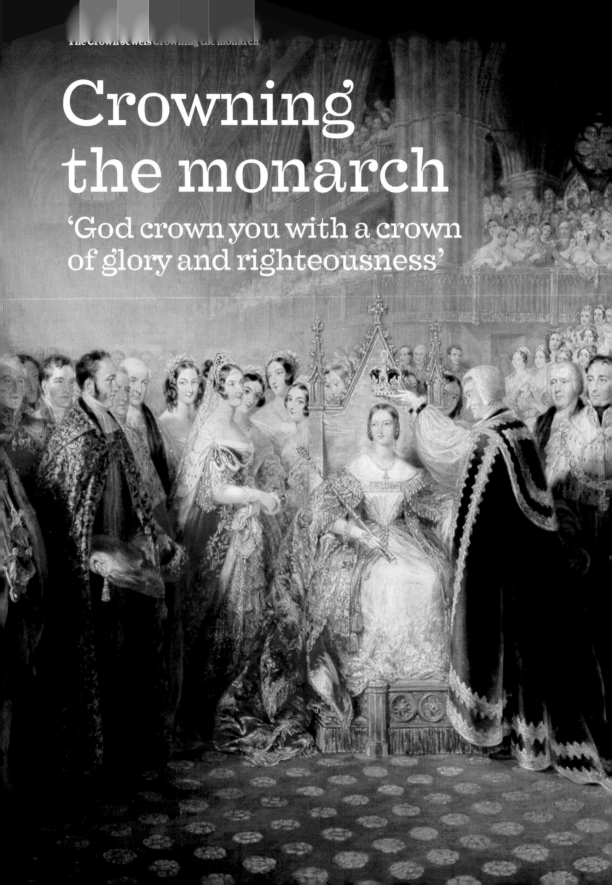

Crowning the monarch

'God crown you with a crown of glory and righteousness'

The crown is the ultimate symbol of royal authority and the moment the Archbishop of Canterbury places the crown on the monarch's head is the climax of the coronation ceremony. Trumpets sound in the Abbey, bells ring out and a 62-gun salute booms from the Tower of London.

The crown has evolved over almost a thousand years to become an object rich in symbolism and meaning. Perhaps uniquely, two crowns came to be used at almost every English coronation: St Edward's Crown and the Imperial State Crown.

The climax of the coronation ceremony, the moment of crowning, is highlighted in this oil painting by Edmund Thomas Paris, *The Coronation of Queen Victoria*, 1838.

Coronation

St Edward's Crown, 1661, is only ever used at the moment of crowning itself. This solid gold crown was made for the coronation of Charles II in 1661 and replaced the medieval crown, melted down in 1649, which was believed to date back to the 11th-century royal saint, Edward the Confessor.

From 1661 until the early 20th century, this crown was only ever adorned with hired stones, which were rented for the duration of the coronation and then returned. In 1911, the crown was permanently set with semi-precious stones for the coronation of George V. At the same time it was made lighter, although it is still very heavy, weighing 2.23kg (nearly 5lb). For this reason St Edward's Crown was not worn but carried in the coronation procession for over 200 years from the reign of Queen Anne.

St. Edward's Crown, 1661, only ever used for the act of crowning a new monarch. It is the most important crown in the Coronation Regalia.

The Coronation Crown of George IV✠, 1821 (see page 59 and 61), was made especially for what the King himself described as his 'gorgeous and extravagant coronation'. For the first time the Crown Jewellers, Rundell, Bridge and Rundell, used open settings to reveal the true brilliance of the 12,314 diamonds. However, the stones had to be hired, at a cost of 10 per cent of their value, and in spite of the King's best efforts to persuade Parliament to buy them, the diamonds were returned and the crown was never used again.

When George IV's 18-year-old niece came to the throne in 1837 a new crown was needed. **Queen Victoria's Crown**✠, 1838, was uniquely intended to do double duty as both a coronation crown and a state crown. It was set with coloured gems removed from its predecessor, George I's State Crown (see page 35).

Above
The Crown of Frederick, Prince of Wales, 1728 is displayed beside the prince in this full-length portrait painted by Jean-Baptiste Van Loo in 1742.

Left
The single-arched Crown of George, Prince of Wales, 1901-2.

The Acclamation

At the moment the monarch is crowned, all the princes, princesses, lords and ladies in the congregation put on their own crowns and coronets and shout out 'God Save the Queen [or King]'.

The **Crown of George, Prince of Wales**, 1901-2, was made in silver-gilt for the Prince (later King George V) to wear at the coronation of his parents, Edward VII and Queen Alexandra. It has one arch rather than two on a king or queen's crown. As decreed by Charles II in 1677: 'the son and heir apparent of the Crown… shall use and bear his coronet composed of crosses and fleurs de Lis with one arch and in the midst a ball and cross'.

The solid gold **Crown of Frederick, Prince of Wales**, 1728, was not worn to his father, George II's, coronation as Frederick had stayed in Hanover, in Germany, to co-ordinate the celebrations there. Frederick's son, later George III, and his grandson, the Prince Regent (George IV), both used the crown. It was carried on a cushion at the State Opening of Parliament to show that the prince did not yet reign.

The Enthroning and Homage

In the final act of the coronation the most senior lords help the monarch move from the ancient St Edward's Chair to a raised throne. The monarch receives oaths of allegiance from the clergy and then the nobles in the Act of Homage, when they used to kiss the royal hand. During this time the General Pardon was proclaimed (when the sovereign pardoned the populace) and coins or medals were flung into the congregation, which could lead to an unseemly scramble.

These crowns are displayed in the Martin Tower as part of the exhibition **Crowns and Diamonds**. This tells the story of how crowns have changed over time and the impact of the arrival of some of the greatest diamonds.

Crowning a queen consort

If a king is married when he comes to the throne his wife is usually anointed and crowned in a short ceremony after the Homage. The last queen consort to have her own coronation was Anne Boleyn, Henry VIII's second wife, in 1533.

When the Italian **Mary of Modena** was crowned alongside James II in 1685 she was the first queen since the Interregnum to require her own regalia and had three gold crowns made: her **diadem** (jewelled headband) to wear on the way to the coronation, a coronation crown (now in the Museum of London) and a **state crown** for other ceremonial occasions. They are rather small and were intended to be worn perched at the back of the head in the continental fashion. The state crown and diadem were adorned with hired diamonds and pearls for the coronation and are today set with rock crystal and cultured pearls.

When Queen Adelaide, consort of William IV, came to the throne at the 'Penny Coronation' in 1831, she insisted on a new consort's crown, in spite of her husband's determination to cut costs. **Queen Adelaide's Crown**✳, 1831, was made of gold and set with diamonds and coloured stones broken from personal royal jewellery at her own expense.

The most famous and spectacular diamonds have passed from one queen's crown to the next. In 1902 Queen Alexandra, consort of Queen Victoria's oldest son, Edward VII, wore the celebrated Koh-i-Nûr diamond from India (see page 49) in a coronation crown for the first time. **Queen Alexandra's Crown**✳, which incorporated a further 3,688 diamonds, has eight half-arches that are typical of crowns in her homeland, Denmark. The crown was only worn for the coronation and is today set with paste stones.

Below
Queen Mary of Modena's State Crown (right) and Diadem, 1685, worn by the queen consort of James II.

Queen Mary's Crown, 1911, was the next to hold the Koh-i-Nûr, and also two of the diamonds cut from the enormous South African Cullinan Diamond (see page 49). Queen Mary had her crown adapted so that these three great diamonds could be worn as jewellery, and replaced with glass paste whilst the crown remained at the Tower of London. The arches – inspired by Queen Alexandra's Crown – could also be removed so that it could be worn as a circlet.

Today the Koh-i-Nûr is set in the most recent queen consort's crown, the **Crown of Queen Elizabeth The Queen Mother**, 1937. This platinum crown is set with 2,800 diamonds, most of them formerly Queen Victoria's, including the 17-carat diamond set below the Koh-i-Nûr, given to her by the Sultan of Turkey in thanks for Britain's support during the Crimean War.

 These crowns are displayed in the Martin Tower as part of the exhibition **Crowns and Diamonds**. This tells the story of how crowns have changed over time and the impact of the arrival of some of the greatest diamonds.

Top left
Queen Alexandra, wife of Edward VII, in her coronation robes and crown set with the Koh-i-Nûr diamond, 1902.

Top
After first adorning Queen Alexandra's Crown, 1902, the celebrated Koh-i-Nûr diamond was then set in Queen Mary's Crown, 1911. It could be removed for the Queen to wear as jewellery.

Above
The Crown of Queen Elizabeth The Queen Mother, 1937, now bears this famous diamond, set in the centre of the front cross.

State Crowns

The Imperial State Crown, 1937, is the crown the monarch exchanges for St Edward's Crown at the end of the coronation ceremony. Before the Civil War the ancient coronation crown was always kept at Westminster Abbey and the monarch needed another crown to wear when leaving the Abbey. It is also used on formal occasions, most notably the annual State Opening of Parliament. The state crown has always been permanently set with much larger – and usually coloured – jewels. Its name refers to the arches with which this crown is closed, chosen in the 15th century to demonstrate that England was not subject to any other earthly power.

The Imperial State Crown is the third replacement made since 1660, and is a near replica of Queen Victoria's Crown (see page 28). Although one of the newer items in the regalia, it holds some of the most historic jewels in the collection, which have attracted many legends (see pages 36-39).

The Imperial State Crown, 1937. This is the 'busiest' crown of the collection; it is worn at the conclusion of the coronation ceremony, as well as on state occasions such as the annual State Opening of Parliament.

Some of these celebrated jewels were earlier set in **George I's State Crown**✳, 1715, which was last worn at the coronation of William IV in 1831, as an economy measure by this most prudent of kings. In contrast, George II previously had it specially set with over £100,000 worth of diamonds for his coronation, equivalent to many millions today.

Two other crowns were made to be worn in place of the Imperial State Crown in special circumstances. **Queen Victoria's Small Diamond Crown**, 1870, was designed as a more modest and appropriate crown to be worn with her widow's veil after the untimely death of her husband, Prince Albert. The tiny diamond and silver crown, only 9.4cm (3.7in) high, was often worn by the Queen in her later years and was finally placed on her coffin.

Victoria's grandson, George V, inherited the title Emperor of India, but as the regalia are not allowed out of the country, the **Imperial Crown of India**, 1911, was made specially for him to wear at the Delhi Durbar, or 'Court of Delhi' in December 1911 (see page 51).

Top left
Queen Victoria's Small Diamond Crown, 1870, was designed as a more modest crown to be worn with her widow's veil after the early death of Prince Albert.

Top right
The Imperial Crown of India, 1911, set with fabulous gems from India and other countries, has only been worn once.

Above
The newly crowned Queen Elizabeth II, wearing the Imperial State Crown and carrying the Orb and Sceptre, enters Buckingham Palace after the Coronation, 2 June 1953.

Anatomy of a crown

The Imperial State Crown is perhaps best known for its major stones, either for their special interest or their immense value. Made for the coronation of George VI in 1937, it contains many of the jewels that adorned crowns from previous centuries, many with fascinating legends attached.

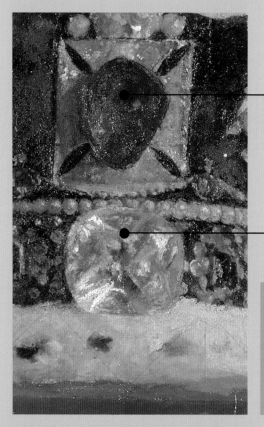

The Black Prince's Ruby
(see overleaf)

Cullinan II (see overleaf)

Jewels
2,868 diamonds
17 sapphires
11 emeralds
269 pearls
4 rubies

Height
31.5cm (12.4in)

Weight
1.006kg
(32oz 7dwt)
excluding wire
frame, cap and
ermine band

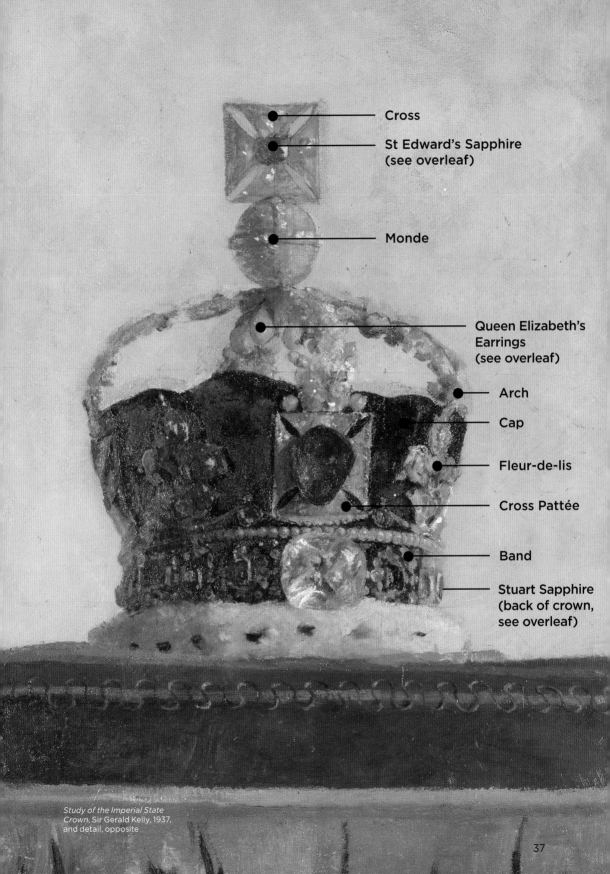

Cross

St Edward's Sapphire
(see overleaf)

Monde

Queen Elizabeth's
Earrings
(see overleaf)

Arch

Cap

Fleur-de-lis

Cross Pattée

Band

Stuart Sapphire
(back of crown,
see overleaf)

*Study of the Imperial State
Crown*, Sir Gerald Kelly, 1937,
and detail, opposite

St Edward's Sapphire

According to legend, this stone was originally set in a ring belonging to Edward the Confessor (1042-66). The saintly king gave the ring away when he was approached by a beggar. The ring was later returned to the King by two pilgrims who met St John the Evangelist in Syria. He told them he had received the ring from the King, while disguised as a beggar, and asked them to return it with the message that the King would join him in Paradise in six months' time.

Queen Elizabeth's Earrings

These four large drop-shaped pearls have become associated with the seven pearls that Catherine de Medici received from Pope Clement VII on her marriage to Henry II of France in 1533. She later gave them to her daughter-in-law, Mary, Queen of Scots, and after her imprisonment they were allegedly sold to Elizabeth I. It is claimed that three of the pearls were later set in Charles II's state crown and were reset in subsequent state crowns. However, despite this romantic tale, at least two of these pearls were in fact added to the Crown Jewels in the early 19th century.

Below left
St Edward the Confessor holding the sapphire ring which was miraculously returned to him. Detail from *The Wilton Diptych*, c1400 made for Richard II.

Below right
Queen Elizabeth I c1588, attributed to George Gower. At least two of the pearls worn by Elizabeth I were added to the Imperial State Crown in the early 19th century.

The Black Prince's Ruby

In the cross at the front of the crown is the very large and irregular 'Black Prince's Ruby', which is not actually a ruby but a balas or spinel, a semi-precious stone. According to legend the stone was owned by the Moors in Spain before it came into the hands of Don Pedro the Cruel, King of Castile. He gave it to Edward, Prince of Wales (known as the Black Prince) in 1367, after the Prince fought for the King and defeated his rival, Henry the Bastard, at the battle of Nájera. It is first recorded in the state crown at the time of James II's coronation in 1685, but does appear to have been shaped and polished much earlier. At the time it was believed to be a true ruby and 'esteemed worth Ten Thousand Pounds'.

Cullinan II

A much more recent addition to the Crown Jewels is the 317.40 carat Cullinan II Diamond (or Second Star of Africa), one of the largest top-quality diamonds ever cut (see page 42).

The Stuart Sapphire

Mounted on the back of the Imperial State Crown, 1937, is the magnificent Stuart Sapphire. This stone was reputedly smuggled out of the country by James II when he fled to France in 1688 during the Glorious Revolution. After his death, it passed to his son, James Stuart, the 'Old Pretender' and then to his grandson Cardinal Henry, Duke of York, brother of 'Bonnie Prince' Charles Edward Stuart. It later came into the possession of George IV, when Prince Regent, and was set into Queen Victoria's Crown in 1838. The sapphire was moved to the back of the crown in 1909 to accommodate Cullinan II.

The Cullinan Diamond

Late one January afternoon in 1905, as the sun was setting, Frederick Wells, Surface Manager of the Premier Mine in the Transvaal Colony (now part of South Africa), was alerted to a shiny object glinting in the steep wall of the mine, just catching the sun's dying rays. Suspecting a practical joker had embedded a piece of glass, he scaled the wall... and pulled out an enormous diamond.

Cullinan I, shown actual size. Weighing 530.2 carats, this magnificent stone is still the largest top-quality cut diamond in the world. In 1910 it was set in the Sovereign's Sceptre with Cross at the request of George V.

The Cullinan Diamond, named after Thomas Cullinan, the mine's chairman, weighed 3,106 carats (1.33lbs) and caused an international sensation. It was the largest diamond ever found. Thought by some to have been part of a still larger stone, on account of a smooth cleavage on one side, rumours abounded of a 'second half' but none was found. Wells was quoted as receiving $10,000 for finding the stone.

The Cullinan Diamond was initially put on display at the Standard Bank in Johannesburg before being sent to England. As security was an obvious issue, a decoy was sent on a heavily guarded ship while the real diamond was sent, insured, by ordinary parcel post! Both arrived safely.

Once in London, buyers were sought for the stone, but none were found. In 1907, at the suggestion of General Louis Botha, Prime Minister of the Transvaal, the diamond was purchased from the Premier Mine Company by the Transvaal Government for £150,000. It was presented to King Edward VII on his 66th birthday, 'as a token of loyalty and attachment of the people of Transvaal to His Majesty's person and Throne'.

The diamond was entrusted to Scotland Yard – the Metropolitan Police headquarters – for safe-keeping until negotiations regarding the cutting of the stone were complete. In 1908 the stone was taken to Amsterdam to be cut by the celebrated firm of Asscher. Prior to the cleaving, a small party, including the manager of the diamond mine and three members of the Asscher family, visited the Jewel House at the Tower of London to look at ways of using the diamond. All agreed that the head of the Sovereign's Sceptre was the most suitable site.

After several practice runs on models, using tools specially made for the task (which can be seen on display in the Martin Tower), the first blow to cleave this massive stone was finally struck on 10 February 1908. The steel cleaving knife broke on impact. The diamond was successfully split by a second blow. Contrary to popular myth, Joseph Asscher, who conducted the procedure, did not faint afterwards. He later remarked that 'No Asscher would faint over an operation on a diamond. He's much more likely to open a bottle of champagne.'

Above
William McHardy, General Manager of the Premier Mine, holding the Cullinan diamond in its original state. He is flanked by Thomas Cullinan (left) and Frederick Wells (right), who prised the stone from the mine wall.

The first two cuts created three stones: the two biggest were to become Cullinan I (530.20 carats) and Cullinan II (317.40 carats), the two largest cut diamonds in the world for many years. The cutting and polishing processes which took three men, working 14 hours a day, eight months to complete, produced nine major stones (Cullinan I-IX), 96 small brilliants and 9 carats of unpolished fragments and resulted in a weight loss of 65.25 per cent.

Cullinan I and II were formally presented to Edward VII on 21 November 1908 and exhibited at the Tower of London two days later as 'The Star of Africa' and the 'Second Star of Africa', while most of the other stones were given to Asscher's in return for their services. Edward VII immediately bought Cullinan VI from Asscher's as a gift for Queen Alexandra and the remaining major stones were bought by the Transvaal Government and subsequently presented to Queen Mary in 1911.

After Edward VII's death in 1910 his son, George V, had Cullinan I inserted in the head of the Sovereign's Sceptre (below left), as originally intended and the transformed sceptre attracted a great deal of attention at his coronation the following year. Cullinan II was set in the front band of the Imperial State Crown in 1909, where it remains in the most recently made version (see page 34). However, both Cullinan I and II could be clipped together and worn as a large and impressive pendant and were used in this way by Queen Alexandra and Queen Mary.

Queen Mary wore Cullinan III and IV in her coronation crown in 1911 (see page 33) and thereafter used them hooked together as a pendant. When she accompanied her husband, George V, to his first State Opening of Parliament on 6 February 1911 she withdrew Cullinan I and II from the Jewel House and wore all four together: Cullinan I and II on her garter sash and III and IV as a pendant on a necklace. Today, Cullinan III and IV (known affectionately within the Royal family as 'the chips') form part of a magnificent brooch worn by Queen Elizabeth II. Cullinan I and II are part of the Crown Jewels but the remainder of the Cullinan stones belong to The Queen's personal jewellery collection.

Left
The Sovereign's Sceptre with Cross, 1661, which was transformed by the addition of the magnificent Cullinan I diamond in 1910.

Above
An official photograph of Queen Mary taken on 6th February 1911, weighed down gloriously with four of the Cullinan diamonds; two on her sash and two below her necklace.

Coronation portrait of George V, 1911. The King is holding the recently transformed Sovereign's Sceptre with Cross, with the enormous Cullinan I diamond.

'I was there...'

The coronation of a new sovereign has always generated great excitement and a desire to participate in the event. While those lucky enough to have received an invitation watch the ceremony inside Westminster Abbey (although not always with the best view), huge crowds line the route of the procession and congregate outside Buckingham Palace trying to catch a glimpse of the new king or queen. In 1953 the coronation was televised for the first time. Over 20 million people in the UK watched the ceremony and for many it was their first experience of television. Here are some eyewitness accounts of past coronations.

Opposite
Eager to catch a glimpse of the newly crowned Queen Elizabeth II in 1953, huge numbers of spectators patiently lined the processional route, and sought unusual vantage points. It was one of the coldest June days on record, but the constant rain did not dampen spirits.

Left
The Coronation of George V; Edward Prince of Wales doing homage by Laurits Regner Tuxen, 1911-13.

Samuel Pepys, diarist

'I sat from past 4 till 11 before the King came in'

Present at the coronation of Charles II, 23 April 1661

'... about 4 I rose and got to the Abbey, where I followed Sir J. Denham, the Surveyor, with some company that he was leading in. And with much ado, by the favour of Mr. Cooper, his man, did get up into a great scaffold across the North end of the Abbey, where with a great deal of patience I sat from past 4 till 11 before the King came in.'

'... the King passed through all the ceremonies of the Coronation, which to my great grief I and most in the Abbey could not see'.

Lord Greville, politician

'Continual difficulty and embarrassment'

Present at the coronation of Queen Victoria, 28 June 1838

'The different actors in the ceremonial were very imperfect in their parts, and had neglected to rehearse them. Nobody knew what was to be done except the Archbishop and Lord John Thynne [Sub-Dean of Westminster] (who had rehearsed), Lord Willoughby (who is experienced in these matters) and the Duke of Wellington, and consequently there was a continual difficulty and embarrassment, and the Queen never knew what she was to do next. They made her leave her chair and enter into St Edward's chapel before the prayers were concluded, much to the discomfiture of the Archbishop. She said to John Thynne, 'Pray tell me what I am to do, for they don't know'; and at the end, when the orb was put into her hand, she said to him, 'What am I to do with it?' 'Your Majesty is to carry it, if you please, in your hand.' 'Am I?' she said; 'it is very heavy'.

Above
Samuel Pepys by John Hayls, 1666.

Below
A view from Buckingham Palace of the royal coach as it passes the Victoria memorial during the coronation parade of George VI on 12 May 1937.

King George V

'I nearly broke down'

Diary entry for his coronation, 22 June 1911

'Today was indeed a great & memorable day in our lives & one we can never forget, but it brought back to me many sad memories of 9 years ago, when the beloved Parents were crowned... The service in the Abbey was most beautiful, but it was a terrible ordeal. It was grand, yet simple & dignified and went without a hitch. I nearly broke down when dear David [the King's son] came to do homage to me, as it reminded me so much when I did the same thing to beloved Papa, he did it so well.'

The Queen, when Princess Elizabeth, aged 11

'Grannie and I were looking to see how many more pages to the end…'

Extract from an account of the coronation of her parents George VI and Queen Elizabeth, 12 May 1937

'I thought it all very, very wonderful and I expect the Abbey did, too. The arches and beams at the top were covered with a sort of haze of wonder as Papa was crowned, at least I thought so.'

'... When Mummy was crowned and all the peeresses put on their coronets it looked wonderful to see arms and coronets hovering in the air and then the arms disappear as if by magic. Also the music was lovely and the band, the orchestra and the new organ all played beautifully.'

'... At the end the service got rather boring as it was all prayers. Grannie [Queen Mary] and I were looking to see how many more pages to the end, and we turned one more and then I pointed to the word at the bottom of the page and it said "Finis". We both smiled at each other and turned back to the service.'

David Starkey, historian

'It was the first time that I had seen television – or a monarch'

'On 2 June 1953, I, then a boy of eight in my Sunday best, gathered along with countless millions more to watch the coronation on a neighbour's television set which had been bought specially for the occasion. It was the first time that I had seen television – or a monarch. And I have never forgotten it.'

'... [Queen] Elizabeth's fear had been that television would trivialize or vulgarize the ceremony. She need not have worried. Instead, the mellifluous, silken-tongued Richard Dimbleby delivered a commentary whose stately language complemented and occasionally outdid the text of the service itself.'

Top
Standing beside her grandmother, the dowager Queen Mary, a young Princess Elizabeth attends the coronation of her parents George VI and Queen Elizabeth on 12 May 1937.

Above
For the first time in history, the coronation ceremony of 1953 was broadcast on television to an audience of countless millions. For many it was their first experience of television, an enduring memory shared with family and friends.

India and the Crown Jewels

Amin Jaffer, formerly Senior Curator in the Department of Asian Art at the Victoria & Albert Museum, explores the origins of some of the most extraordinary gems in the collection.

India was considered the 'Jewel in the Crown' of the British Empire in the period between 1858 and 1947, a metaphor for the prestige and importance of this ancient civilisation above all the other colonies that constituted Britain's far-flung imperial possessions.

Opposite
A detail showing the cross and monde of the Imperial Crown of India, 1911. The crown was adorned with many precious gems from the Indian subcontinent.

Above
The 16th-century Mughal emperor Babur, who is said to have described the Koh-i-Nûr diamond as 'being worth half of the daily expense of the whole world'.

The 'Jewel in the Crown' also reflects India's position as the home of many of the world's greatest precious stones. Indeed, before the middle of the 18th century, the subcontinent was the only known source of diamonds, in addition to which rubies, sapphires and pearls were also abundantly available in the region. With the gradual subjugation of India to British interests, precious commodities – especially jewels – naturally flowed to British coffers, both as war booty and as tokens of homage from the many native princes who sought to appease their new imperial overlords.

The Koh-i-Nûr

In both east and west great jewels have always changed hands from one ruler to another, following the holders of power. This characterises the history of the Koh-i-Nûr, the most significant Indian diamond in the Crown Jewels. The history of this magnificent stone is rich in myth and anecdote. Originating in the famed Golconda diamond mines of the Deccan, in central southern India, the stone is perhaps the large diamond won by the Mughal prince Babur (1483-1531) in his conquest of northern India and which he described as being worth 'half of the daily expense of the whole world'. The diamond was taken from the Mughal treasury by the Iranian warrior Nadir Shah (1698-1747) when he sacked Delhi in 1739. Desperate to find the legendary stone, he learned that the vanquished Mughal emperor kept it secreted within the folds of his turban. Offering to exchange turbans with the ruler in a ceremonial act of friendship, Nadir Shah obtained his prize. On finally seeing the diamond he said in astonishment: 'Koh-i-Nûr' or 'Mountain of Light', giving the stone its present name.

Nadir Shah was killed in 1747 and the diamond changed hands again, to the Durani rulers of Afghanistan, the last of whom offered it in 1813 to Maharaja Ranjit Singh (1780-1839), the ruler of the Punjab. It eventually passed to his successor, the young Maharaja Duleep Singh (1838-93), from whom it was taken when the Punjab was annexed by the East India Company in 1849. The treaty that marked the end of the Anglo-Sikh Wars, specified that 'The gem called the Koh-i-noor... shall be surrendered... to the Queen of England'. It travelled to London in its original setting, as the centre-piece of a bazu-band, or upper armband, set in gold, the reverse side richly enamelled.

Queen Victoria received the stone with pleasure, noting that although it was 'badly cut' it was 'indeed a proud trophy'. The Indian style of faceting the great diamond did not achieve the sparkle so sought after in European jewellery of the period. The Koh-i-Nûr was accordingly removed from its setting and transformed from a 186-carat rose-cut to a cushion-shaped brilliant of 105.60 carats, the Duke of Wellington helping to cut the first facet. The Queen wore the newly fashioned stone variously as a brooch and in a circlet; on her death the stone became part of the Crown Jewels.

Given its tempestuous history, the Koh-i-Nûr was thought to mean bad luck if worn by a man. On Queen Victoria's death, the stone was therefore set into Queen Alexandra's Crown (see page 32), made by Carrington & Company. Following the convention that each queen consort was made a new crown for her coronation, the stone successively adorned the crown of Queen Mary, 1911, and that of Queen Elizabeth The Queen Mother, 1937, where it remains today (see page 33).

Left
The Koh-i-Nûr, cut in the traditional 'rose' style, arrived from India in this enamalled gold armlet.

Above
When the young Queen Victoria received the Koh-i-Nûr she did not consider it brilliant enough, so it was soon recut to create more facets. Here she wears the magnificent, newly cut diamond in a brooch.

The Delhi Durbar

In 1876 Queen Victoria adopted the title Empress of India, establishing a bond between herself and the people of the Indian subcontinent. An 'Imperial Assemblage' was held at Delhi at which the title was officially proclaimed by the Viceroy, Lord Lytton, in the presence of India's leading princes. This durbar, or court, was the first of three such spectacular events – the others in 1903 and 1911 commemorating the accession of Edward VII and George V respectively – at which the relationship between the sovereign and India's native princes was most clearly articulated.

On his accession to the throne in 1910, George V decided that he and Queen Mary should be crowned both in Britain and in India. However, the Archbishop of Canterbury considered the idea of a formal Christian coronation ceremony inappropriate for a nation composed largely of Hindus and Muslims. As the Crown Jewels are not permitted to leave the British Isles, another question to be resolved was that of the appropriate regalia to be worn by the monarch in an Indian context. Ultimately, the King entered the durbar arena in Delhi wearing a fabulous new crown made for the occasion and set with 6,002 diamonds and coloured gems of Indian origin: sapphires, rubies and emeralds (the latter actually Colombian, but believed to be Indian at the time).

The Delhi Durbar was held on 12 December 1911, the Government using the event to announce the shift of the capital of British India from Calcutta to New Delhi. Dressed throughout the ceremony in rich coronation robes unsuited to the Indian climate, the King noted in his diary afterwards that he was 'Rather tired after wearing the Crown for 3 hours... it hurt my head as it is pretty heavy'. The Imperial Crown of India was made at the cost of £60,000 and paid for by Indian revenues.

It was worn only once; when George VI ascended the throne in 1937 India was already on its way to Independence and rejected the idea of a coronation durbar.

Following the break-up of British India in 1947, the various successor states entered the British Commonwealth. The national flowers of India and Ceylon (now Sri Lanka) are represented on the stole worn by Queen Elizabeth II at her coronation in 1953 (see page 21). Pakistan and Ceylon contributed towards the 22-carat gold Armills worn by The Queen on that occasion (see page 22).

Above
George V and Queen Mary at the Delhi Durbar of 1911. The royal couple endured over three hours in the Indian sun wearing their English robes of state, with the King getting gradually wearier under the weight of the specially made Imperial Crown of India.

S Moore feat.

The king's feast

The earliest accounts of English coronations mention the king's feast, every bit as important as the preceding religious ceremony in Westminster Abbey.

The coronation banquet, which followed the monarch's return procession to Westminster Hall, became the ultimate public meal. It was an occasion when the king would display his magnificence and generosity to his new subjects. In return, the ruling elite could show their loyalty through acts of personal service at the royal table. The earliest feast described was that of the Saxon king Edgar in 973, who ate at a separate table from his queen, seated with his powerful archbishops. This dignified scene is in stark contrast to his brother Eadwig who, according to legend, broke off from his coronation feast and was discovered in disarray in his chamber with Æthelgifu and Ælfgifu – a mother and her daughter! By the time of Richard I (crowned in 1189) we learn a little more of arrangements for the feast: the coronation crown and vestments were exchanged for lighter ones – later known as state crown and robes – and the king was served at breakfast by his barons.

The scale of the medieval feast could be gargantuan: more than 5,000 dishes and 900 cups were served on one occasion, which gives some idea of the number of guests. By the coronation of Edward II in 1308 consumption of wine had reached an intoxicating 1,000 casks. The manner of serving all this food and drink was equally impressive: at his coronation wine flowed from a fountain.

Opposite
An engraving from Francis Sandford's commemorative book *The History of the Coronation of King James II* (London, 1687) showing the King, Queen and members of the nobility enjoying the coronation banquet in Westminster Hall on 23 April, 1685.

Left
Detail from the top of the Plymouth Fountain, a gorgeous table centrepiece that originally spouted rosewater (see overleaf).

Left
The Plymouth Fountain, mid-17th century, given to Charles II by the people of the city as an act of allegiance to the monarch following the Civil War.

Right
The Queen Elizabeth Salt, 1572, is the oldest surviving banqueting plate in the jewel house, apart from the Coronation Spoon (see page 20).

An echo of this is the surviving **Plymouth Fountain**, a gift to Charles II from the city of Plymouth at his Restoration in 1660, but actually made in Hamburg in Germany, possibly by Peter Oehr I. Originally, perfumed water was pumped into its four basins from small pipes held by figures of Poseidon and water nymphs on the central column.

By the Tudor period guests devoured elaborate *subtleties* – sculpted food often decorated with the monarch's badges. Although coronation menus for this period do not survive, we know that at Anne Boleyn's banquet (1533) there were 'ships made of wax marvellous gorgeous to behold'. This was the peak of such theatricality at coronations. Later monarchs were restrained by dwindling finances and fashions for plainer food.

Over time rituals developed around this feast. Some survived like relics of a long lost age such as the arrival of the King's Champion (see below). They were so numerous that a Court of Claims was held before every coronation to determine who had the right to carry out such lucrative royal services.

The banquet followed the return procession from the Abbey back to Westminster Hall. The monarch's arrival was announced by trumpeters above the north door and the king and queen moved to the high dais at the far end where they sat behind a long table for all to see. Typically, the first course would be led down the hall by the Lord Great Chamberlain, the Constable and Earl Marshal, all riding on horseback. (They had the unenviable task of riding out backward, a feat that only the Duke of Wellington could manage at the banquet of George IV.) This was followed by the extraordinary sight of the King's Champion, for centuries a member of the Dymoke family, riding in full armour, and throwing down his gauntlet three times on behalf of the monarch. The unchallenged champion was then toasted by the king and received his gold cup as his fee. Minstrels sang during the second course and more gifts and toasts were made after the void, or dessert. Throughout proceedings the Earl Marshal kept order from the saddle. This was no mere formality; at the banquet for George II crowds let in to consume the leftovers took everything in sight and then fell to blows.

Banqueting plate in the Jewel House

The banquet demanded a splendid array of gold and silver plate, although these have proved far less durable than the customs. Apart from the Coronation Spoon, the banqueting plate in the Jewel House today largely dates from the Restoration of Charles II in 1660, following the melting down of early plate during the Interregnum.

The chief item at the king's table was the salt, its significance originating from the time when salt was a luxury commodity and cautiously guarded for fear of poisoning. Charles II issued an ordinance that declared that once the salt cellar was on the table everyone except the diners had to remain standing in respect. The **Queen Elizabeth Salt**, 1572, is the oldest silver-gilt plate in the Jewel House apart from the Coronation Spoon, probably made by Elizabeth I's most skilled silversmith, Affabel Partridge, although it appears to have been acquired by Charles II. The associations are entirely appropriate as it is superbly ornamented with figures of heroines and virtuous women, and also engraved with a Tudor rose.

One of the showiest pieces – recalling Tudor subtleties – is the **Exeter Salt**, c1630, also given to Charles II in 1660 as a gift of allegiance by the city of Exeter. It is in the shape of a castle on a rocky mound, with salt hidden in each turret and drawers for spices. Sometimes linked to the White Tower, it was actually made in Hamburg by Johann Hass and its 73 gems and enamelled English emblems were probably added when it was given to the King.

The other principal royal banquet was held by the Knights of the Garter each year on or around the feast of their patron saint, St George. Charles II was crowned on St George's Day (23 April) 1661 and it is little wonder that he seems to have honoured this ancient order (founded in 1348) with the large group of **St George's Salts**, 1660-1. Eleven remain of three differing designs, probably ordered to be placed before the 24 knights at the Order of the Garter feast. The brackets to hold the missing covers were once thought to be legs and for years they were shown to visitors upside down! A knightly figure surmounts the remaining covers.

Top
St. George's Salts, 1660-1. The salts are thought to have been made for the annual feast of the Order of the Garter held shortly before the coronation of Charles II on St George's Day, 1661.

Above
The Exeter Salt, c1630. Concealed within the tower and turrets of this extraordinary piece of royal tableware are seven separate wells for salt. In the main body of the castle are three deep drawers which may have held spices.

There are a number of wine flagons and smaller tankards from this period, such as the pair with wild bacchanalian scenes by the German goldsmith Hans Lembrecht III, used on the buffet at Charles II's coronation. Others were made to hold communion wine, a necessity of the Anglican Church where the whole congregation took part.

The latest banqueting plate is also the greatest and a fitting tribute to its first owner, George IV, who was the last king to hold a coronation banquet (see page 58). Conceived as a giant ice bucket for wine, the huge **Wine Cistern,** or cooler (large enough to hold 144 bottles), was designed as a glorious rococo shell in a rockpool.

Later used as a vessel for hot punch, it is also known as the Grand Punch Bowl. It was created by the Crown Jewellers, Rundell, Bridge and Rundell, who over his short reign (1820-30), helped the king run up enormous debts. Alas his own excessive diet meant he did not survive long enough to enjoy this, the largest piece of English plate.

Below
Over 1m (3ft) wide and weighing around 248kg (546lb), the Grand Punch Bowl is a fitting testament to the excesses of George IV, one of our most flamboyant monarchs.

'A blaze of diamonds'

After spending ten frustrating years as Prince Regent, King George IV was determined to put on a coronation show to be remembered.

Opposite
The Banquet at the Coronation of George IV by George Jones, 1821 with the King's Champion in full armour in the foreground.

Above
George IV's official state portrait by Sir Thomas Lawrence, 1821. His extraordinary coronation crown is resting on the table next to him (see page 61)

Prince George had waited a decade in the wings as his father George III wrestled with the symptoms of porphyria. When he finally died in 1820 the country had to wait another agonising year for an opportunity to celebrate the accession when the new king's estranged wife, Queen Caroline, reappeared. He was forced to postpone the event in order to try to divorce her, which he did in the most public and acrimonious manner. However, on the day, his coronation was probably one of the most lavish ever seen.

It was a Romantic fabrication of ancient tradition and medieval revivalism, completely in tune with the age of Walter Scott, JMW Turner and the elder Pugin, enhanced by the creative showmanship of the Prince who had built the Brighton Pavilion. The notoriously profligate 'Prinny' planned his coronation in immense detail and inevitably at vast expense. The final cost was over £243,000, more than 25 times the cost of his father's coronation and some £10 million at today's values.

It was a glorious pageant in which every participant was provided with fantastic costumes, inspired by the courts of Elizabeth I and the early Stuarts. The King wore silver doublet and hose, with a train that took the sons of eight lords to bear. During the procession he wore a curious plumed 'Spanish hat' over his usual black wig and a magnificent new circlet of diamonds (see front cover flap), still worn by The Queen today.

For the crowning itself George abandoned his ancestor George I's crown (see page 31) and devised a brilliant new one set with over 12,000 diamonds, which were hired at 10 per cent per annum of their value – some £65,000 (when a family might survive on £30 per year) to obtain the largest possible stones. Westminster Abbey and Westminster Hall were given a makeover in the Gothic style and galleries were built to accommodate guests whose numbers were increased to 4,656. This was only achieved by reducing the width of the seats allocated to the nobility!

On a hot and sultry 18 July, bells pealed at the start of the last ever procession on foot from Westminster Hall to the Abbey. The whole occasion notoriously nearly came unstuck when Queen Caroline, whom the King had barred, arrived at the door of the Abbey demanding to be admitted and crowned. A fracas ensued between her supporters and the boxers hired as doormen, who turned her away, to a mixture of jeers and cries of 'shame' from the crowd.

The coronation ceremony itself largely followed tradition, though the King added to the pomp by including Handel's Hallelujah Chorus for his arrival at the Abbey. The impression it made on observers depended on personal standpoints, as King George had as many detractors as admirers. The artist Benjamin Haydon thought the King 'showed like some gorgeous bird from the East', whilst the acerbic Mrs Arbuthnot thought him 'excessively pale and tired', and indeed the very overweight King used 19 handkerchiefs in the heat. Those close to the coronation theatre were appalled to see this sentimental monarch openly ogling his mistress, Lady Conyngham, nearby.

An even greater contrast of grandeur and farce took place in the last ever coronation banquet in Westminster Hall. Both glutton and gourmand, King George made sure his 300 guests left replete. The huge cost of £25,000 for the banquet alone included 160 tureens of turtle soup, 160 dishes of lobster, nearly 8,000lb of beef, 400 calves' feet and 8,400 eggs, washed down with almost 10,000 bottles of wine. However, this most medieval of events was marred by a series of mishaps. The Marquis of Anglesey was meant to present the first course after riding down the hall but could not dismount unaided, as this Napoleonic war veteran was wearing the 'wrong' wooden leg. Peers were mistakenly served a cold collation (a light snack) whilst City Aldermen enjoyed the Peers' venison and turtle. And the last appearance of the King's Champion in full armour on horseback, throwing down the

gauntlet to challengers to the King's title, was diminished by the youth of the deputy champion from the Dymoke family, who rode a horse rather sensibly hired from Astley's circus.

In spite of its excess and lapses into bathos, George IV's coronation was ultimately rather a successful beginning to the reign of this often unpopular monarch. Whilst the King lacked the political power and public acclaim of his father, George III, he certainly knew how to put on a show to be remembered. But his 'flirtation with grandeur', as one historian has put it, would never again be repeated by his successors.

The Coronation Crown of George IV, 1821

A key part of George IV's extravagant coronation plans was the design of a new coronation crown. The gold and silver crown frame was constructed in a new way, with open settings that made the frame almost invisible behind the diamonds. The crown was encrusted in an extraordinary 12,314 diamonds. No other monarch has worn George IV's coronation crown, which has remained empty of stones since 1823. The crown frame can be seen displayed in the Martin Tower.

Altar and christening plate

When Charles II was restored to the throne in 1660 an enormous quantity of plate was required, both for his coronation and for his personal use, to replace the many pieces melted down during the Interregnum.

Opposite
Coronation of Queen Victoria by George Hayter, 1839 (detail) with a large array of royal chapel plate displayed on the altar.

Above
Flagon and altar dish depicting the *Supper at Emmaus*, 1691. Both pieces are engraved with the cypher of William and Mary.

Chalices and patens

Holy Communion has always been a crucial part of the coronation ceremony; having received the homage of the congregation, the sovereign kneels at the altar to be given the bread and wine by the Archbishop of Canterbury.

There are some 15 chalices and patens in the collection, which hold the wine and bread respectively, during Communion. These include the only wrought gold pieces of plate in the Jewel House. The solid gold chalice and paten of c1661 were ordered for the coronation of Charles II and have been used at many subsequent coronations. The second gold chalice and paten and small gold paten date from before 1688 and were probably made for Charles's brother, James, Duke of York (the future James II). His arms were later erased and replaced with those of William III and Mary II.

The Last Supper altar dish, 1664

This magnificent altar dish forms the centrepiece on the high altar at Westminster Abbey during the coronation ceremony. It is one of the largest surviving altar dishes of the period being nearly a metre (3ft) in diameter and weighing nearly 13kg (29lb).

The four panels on the border depict the Washing of the Apostles' feet, the Walk to Emmaus, Christ's commission to the Apostles and the Coming of the Holy Ghost. Above the central representation of the Last Supper are the royal arms of James, Duke of York. An almost identical dish made for Charles II in 1660 is in use at the Chapel Royal, St James's Palace.

The altar dish and flagon, 1691

Made specifically for the Chapel of St Peter ad Vincula in the Tower, these pieces are still used each Christmas, Easter and Whitsun (see page 63). They have also been used at every coronation since 1821 and are engraved with the cipher of William III and Mary II.

The collection also includes six monumental **Feathered flagons**, the largest surviving examples of English flagons. Their design may have derived from similar pieces known to have been in Henry VIII's possession. Four were made for Charles II in 1660 and two for the Duke of York in 1664. All are engraved with the Stuart arms.

The great **Altar candlesticks**, c1661, decorated with flowers and foliage, were probably made for Charles II in 1661. They were used at the lying-in-state of Edward VII at Buckingham Palace in 1910.

Opposite
Gold chalices and patens
made for Charles II and his
family after the Restoration.

Above
The Last Supper altar dish,
1664. Almost a metre in
diameter, this huge altar
plate forms the centrepiece
of the high altar in
Westminster Abbey during
the coronation ceremony.

Christening fonts

Charles II Font and Basin, 1660

Although Charles II was unmarried when he came to the throne in 1660, he persuaded the Treasury to pay for a magnificent christening font and basin. His subsequent marriage to Catherine of Braganza produced no children but it is thought that the font was used to christen some of his many illegitimate children. The font was used for royal christenings up to the late 18th century and its last recorded use appears to be for the christening of Princess Charlotte in 1796. The font and basin served as a stand for the Lily Font (right) at the christening of Queen Victoria's son, the Prince of Wales, in 1842, and the basin was used as an altar dish at the coronations of George IV and Queen Victoria.

Christening Basin and Ewer, c1735

First used for the christening of the future King George III in 1738. His father, Frederick, Prince of Wales, had been banished from the court of George II and was denied the use of the Charles II Font. Both pieces are engraved with the royal arms of George III and an inscription recording their use at his christening and at the subsequent christening of his ninth son, Prince Alfred in 1780.

The Lily Font, 1840

The Lily Font was made for the baptism of Queen Victoria's first child, Princess Victoria, in 1840. It was said that the Queen did not care to baptise her children in the Charles II Font because of its links with his illegitimate children. The three coats of arms on the base of the font are all personal royal arms. The Lily Font is still used for royal christenings, together with the ewer of 1735. It was recently used in April 2008 for the christening of Prince Edward's son, Viscount Severn.

Left
Charles II Font and Basin, 1660. Although commissioned by Charles II, the first recorded use of these baptismal pieces was for the christening of James II's son, James Francis Edward, later known as the 'Old Pretender'.

Above
The Lily Font, 1840. The bowl of this delicately worked font is edged by eight open water lilies. The font is still used for royal christenings today.

The Maundy Dish, 1660

Used by the monarch on Maundy Thursday (the Thursday before Easter) for the distribution of specially minted coins, Maundy Money, to a select group of people. The ceremony commemorates that part of the Last Supper where Jesus washed the feet of his disciples and commanded them to love one another. A form of the ceremony has been known in England since about the 6th century, but from the late 17th century until 1931 the monarch played no active role in the service and the Maundy was distributed by the Lord High Almoner. From the reign of Edward III until the 19th century, the provision of a meal and the distribution of gifts of food and clothing formed a traditional part of the ceremony. The washing of the feet of the poor was also a central part of the service until the late 17th century.

The Maundy Money consists of one, two, three and four pence pieces in silver, which are the only British silver coins still made. Since the reign of Henry VI (1422-61), the number of recipients of the Maundy gifts, and the number of coins they receive, has been related to the sovereign's age at the time of the ceremony.

The coins are held in white and red leather purses carried on dishes by Yeomen of the Guard above their heads. A pair of altar dishes c1661 is used to supplement the Maundy Dish. The centre of each is decorated with a crowned rose surrounded by freshwater fish on one dish and saltwater varieties on the other. As the service takes place at a different cathedral each year, the 'freshwater dish' is used at inland cathedrals and the 'saltwater dish' at coastal ones.

Above left
The Maundy Dish, 1660, has been used every year since 1694 to carry the traditional purses of money in the Maundy ceremony.

Above right
Carried by a cohort of Yeoman of the Guard, the Maundy Money makes an appearance at the traditional Maundy service.

The day the Crown Jewels were nearly stolen

Security for these priceless objects has not always been as tight as you might expect!

In the 17th century, the Crown Jewels were kept in a locked storeroom in the Martin Tower, under the care of the elderly Jewel House Keeper Talbot Edwards who lived in rooms above with his family. For a fee, visitors could handle the jewels. One visitor, a clergyman, showed an extremely keen interest, returning several times during the spring of 1671. Under the disguise was 'Colonel' Thomas Blood, a mercenary who had fought in the Civil War.

Blood was a mysterious and contradictory character. He was a violent and reckless adventurer, while at the same time deeply religious, a Nonconformist who claimed to avoid strong drink. Although he had seen some military service, his rank of 'Colonel' was a conceit of his own.

To this day his true motive – or sponsor of his attempt to steal the Crown Jewels – is unknown. He planned the raid meticulously, becoming firm friends of Talbot Edwards during regular visits.

On the morning of 9 May 1671 Blood and his gang arrived early at the Tower. The 'Colonel' was accompanied by his son Thomas, a friend Robert Perot and Richard Halliwell, a well-known thug. Unsuspecting Edwards was only too delighted to show Blood and his friends the jewels, and he led the way downstairs to the storeroom.

Then, while Halliwell stood guard outside the door, Blood and his gang turned on Edwards. They bound the elderly man's hands behind his back and rammed a piece of wood in his mouth. Despite this, Edwards struggled so much that he was stabbed and beaten about the head. Perot stuffed the Orb down his breeches, Blood crushed the State Crown so it would fit under his cloak, and his son Thomas was told to saw the Sovereign's Sceptre in half so as to carry it out in a bag.

So far so good for the villains... and then their luck changed. Talbot Edwards's son appeared unexpectedly, back from the army after several years abroad. He raised the alarm, and Blood's gang made a run for it.

The guards got Perot at once; Blood and his son nearly made it to the gate, shooting behind them as they ran. But soon all the jewel thieves were overpowered.

Even when facing interrogation in the Tower, Blood remained surprisingly calm. He demanded to see the King and was granted an audience.

Some say that with Blood's contacts in the Nonconformist community, the King recognised Blood's value as a spy. Or had he been working as a double agent all along and this was his reward? The truth may never be known, but it is claimed that Blood's 'blarney' won the day and Charles clearly was amused by him. When the King asked Blood what he would do if his life were spared, the Colonel is supposed to have replied 'endeavour to deserve it'.

The King was convinced, somehow. On 18 July, the Secretary of State brought a warrant to the Tower for Blood's release, and by the end of August Blood received a full pardon for all his previous crimes, and a grant of Irish lands worth £500 a year.

After Colonel Blood's attack, the jewels were made marginally more secure behind wooden bars, until a mentally ill woman reached into the case and damaged one of the crowns. Security gradually improved until The Crown Jewels were moved into the highly secure Jewel House in the basement of the Waterloo Block in 1967. The present Jewel House was opened by HM Queen Elizabeth II in 1994.

The story of Colonel Blood's daring escapade is a favourite among visitors to the Tower of London (and our costumed interpreters)! Next time you come to see the Crown Jewels, keep an eye out for suspicious characters lurking near the Jewel House...

Opposite
The 'reckless adventurer'
Thomas Blood, artist unknown.

Four more palaces to explore;
hundreds of stories to discover

Hampton Court Palace

Explore Henry VIII's magnificent palace, then stroll through the elegant Baroque apartments and glorious formal gardens of William III and Mary II. Feel the heat of the vast Tudor Kitchens and the eerie chill of the Haunted Gallery, before you disappear into the fiendish Maze...

Kew Palace and Queen Charlotte's Cottage

Step into this tiny doll's house of a palace and experience the joys and sorrows of King George III and his family through a sound scape and displays of fascinating personal artefacts. Stroll to Queen Charlotte's Cottage, built in 1770, where the royal family enjoyed picnics and peace in a tranquil corner of Kew Gardens.

Open April – October. Entry to Kew Gardens is required to visit Kew Palace and Queen Charlotte's Cottage.

Banqueting House

Walk in the footsteps of a dazzling company of courtiers who once danced, drank and partied beneath Rubens's magnificent painted ceiling. This revolutionary building was created for court entertainments, but is probably most famous for the execution of Charles I in 1649. Spare him a thought as you gaze up at this ravishing painting – one of his last sights on earth...

Kensington Palace

The palace is being transformed – it has been turned inside out and its stories and secrets are being shaken out with the dust. They tell of the lives of beautiful princesses: Diana and Margaret, Victoria, Charlotte and Caroline, Mary and Anne, caught within the strange and mysterious world of the court – a world within a world, governed by its own time and rituals.

We offer an exciting programme of events and exhibitions throughout the year. For more information and details on tickets and how to find us, please visit www.hrp.org.uk

Supporting us

Historic Royal Palaces is the independent charity that looks after the Tower of London, Hampton Court Palace, the Banqueting House, Kensington Palace and Kew Palace. We help everyone explore the story of how monarchs and people have shaped society in some of the greatest palaces ever built.

We receive no funding from the Government or the Crown so we depend on the support of our visitors, members, donors, volunteers and sponsors.

Can you help?

We hope that you have thoroughly enjoyed your visit to the Tower of London and have discovered more about the conservation of this ancient building. Our work goes on; funds will always be needed to protect and maintain the Tower. Any donation that you can spare means this valuable work can continue.

Please call the Development Department **on 0845 389 3003** for more information, or email **development@hrp.org.uk**.

Thank you.

Join us!

Joining Historic Royal Palaces is the perfect way to explore the inside stories of five extraordinary places that helped define our nation's history. What's more, you'll save money and contribute to the important work of conserving the palaces at the same time.

It's amazing value; membership of Historic Royal Palaces means you have the freedom to visit the Tower of London, Hampton Court Palace, the Banqueting House, Kensington Palace and Kew Palace (open April – October) as often as you like. Membership also means you don't have to queue – simply walk in to see, experience and understand what makes us who we are. Other benefits include exclusive members-only events, behind-the-scenes tours and great discounts in our shops and online.

Make a present of the past

Step through the doors of a royal palace and you are surrounded by stories of strategy, intrigue, ambition, romance, devotion and disaster. What more inspiring gift could there be than a Historic Royal Palaces Membership for someone who shares your love of history, amazing buildings, their beautiful contents and gorgeous gardens?

To enquire about becoming a member of Historic Royal Palaces and for more information on the range of benefits you receive, please visit **www.hrp.org.uk** or call **0870 751 5174**.

Acknowledgements

Published by
Historic Royal Palaces
Hampton Court Palace
Surrey KT8 9AU

© Historic Royal Palaces, 2010

ISBN: 978-1-873993-13-2

Written by Sally Dixon-Smith, Sebastian Edwards, Sarah Kilby, Clare Murphy, David Souden, Jane Spooner and Lucy Worsley.

Edited by Clare Murphy, Sarah Kilby and Susan Mennell

Picture procurement by Annie Heron

Designed by McGillan Eves

Printed by Brown, Knight & Truscott Ltd.

Illustrations

All photography of the Crown Jewels by Prudence Cuming Associates © HM Queen Elizabeth II 2001.

Abbreviations: b = bottom, c = centre, l = left, r = right, t = top

De Beers: page 41; Bradford Art Galleries and Museums: pages 28-9; The Bridgeman Art Library: pages 26t (British Library, London, UK/© British Library Board. All Rights Reserved), 60t (Private Collection); By permission of The British Library: page 6; © The British Museum: page 61t; In the collection of The Trustees of the Ninth Duke of Buccleuch's Chattels Fund: pages 16-17; Camera Press, London: page 47b; Reproduced by permission of English Heritage/Heritage Images: page 67r; © Getty Images: pages 9 (2008 Anwar Hussein), 33tl, 35b, 47t; © Guildhall Library, Corporation of London: pages 10-11, 60b; Crown copyright: Historic Royal Palaces: pages 52, 69; Hulton Archive: pages 12r (detail), 27 (detail); © Hulton-Deutsch Collection/CORBIS: page 46b; The Master and Fellows of Magdalene College, Cambridge: page 68; Mary Evans Picture Library/Illustrated London News: pages 42t, 43; Courtesy of the Museum of London: pages 18-19; © National Gallery, London: page 38l; National Portrait Gallery, London: pages 38r, 46t; The Royal Collection © 2009 Her Majesty Queen Elizabeth II: pages 2-3, 7 (detail), 8, 15 (detail), 31r, 36-37, 45, 50t, 58, 59, 62 (detail); © Topham Picturepoint/TopFoto.co.uk: pages 44, 51; V&A Picture Library: page 49.

Front cover flap: © Hulton-Deutsch Collection/CORBIS

Back cover flap: Camera Press, London (Photograph by Cecil Beaton)

Extract from Monarchy by David Starkey, page 47, reproduced by kind permission of HarperCollins Publishers Ltd. © 2005 David Starkey.

Extract from Princess Elizabeth's account of her parents' coronation, page 47, reproduced from the Royal Archives by the permission of Her Majesty Queen Elizabeth II.

The exhibition 'Crowns and Diamonds: the making of the Crown Jewels' has been made possible by the generosity of De Beers. Their contribution is gratefully acknowledged.

Historic Royal Palaces is a registered charity (no. 1068852)

www.hrp.org.uk

Back cover flap
Her Majesty Queen Elizabeth II wearing the Imperial State Crown and holding the Sovereign's Sceptre with Cross and the Sovereign's Orb. Photographed by Cecil Beaton on the day of her coronation, 2 June 1953.